JUPITER

Also by Franklyn M. Branley

JUPITER

KING OF THE GODS, GIANT OF THE PLANETS

Franklyn M. Branley

Diagrams by Leonard D. Dank

LODESTAR BOOKS
E. P. DUTTON   NEW YORK

Photos NASA/JPL

Library of Congress Cataloging in Publication Data

Branley, Franklyn Mansfield.
Jupiter: king of the gods, giant of the planets.
Bibliography: p.
Includes index.
SUMMARY: Presents information accumulated about Jupiter through the centuries, including data collected by Pioneers 10 and 11 and Voyagers 1 and 2, and some of the mythology surrounding this planet.
1. Jupiter (Planet)—Juvenile literature. [1. Jupiter (Planet)] I. Title.
QB661.B7   523.4′5   81-9890
ISBN 0-525-66739-3   AACR2

Published in the United States by E. P. Dutton, Inc., 2 Park Avenue, New York, N.Y. 10016. Published simultaneously in Canada by Clarke, Irwin & Company, Limited, Toronto and Vancouver
Editor: Virginia Buckley   Designer: Trish Parcell
Printed in the U.S.A.
10 9 8 7 6 5 4 3 2

CONTENTS

CHAPTER 1

PLANETS AND STARS

For a hundred thousand years and long before that, men and women have gazed into the star-filled skies. Somewhere along the way a few among these ancestors of ours looked at the stars more carefully than did others. They noticed that, among the countless stars, there were five that changed position. We cannot be sure what very early people thought about them, for there is no written record. But we know they were objects of wonder and curiosity to the Babylonians.

The Babylonians, some five thousand years ago, lived in the Mideast, in the valley of the Tigris and Euphrates rivers. On a map you'll see that the area is now called Iraq. For hundreds of years the region was a center of learning, which was passed on in a kind of primitive form of writing called cuneiform.

From records set down by the Babylonians, we know how they felt about the roving stars. They considered them important gods who lived in the sky, gods called Nebo, Ishtar, Nergal, Marduk, and Ninib—or, as we would say after the Romans, Mercury, Venus, Mars, Jupiter, and Saturn.

Gods were important to early peoples. Gods controlled crops, the rain, the seasons. There were gods of battle and of peace, of the kitchen and the harvest, of good luck and bad luck. Marduk was the Babylonians' chief god, the one who created heaven and earth, the stars in the heavens, and even many of the lesser gods.

Thus the Babylonians named the chief of these roving stars after Marduk. They had noted that it often became very bright and moved slowly, majestically, among the other stars. It could be seen dominating the sky for month after month. It seemed suitable to name the giant of the roving stars after the king of the gods.

Centuries later the center of learning had shifted to Greece. The Greek people also had hundreds of gods to whom they turned for guidance and direction. The gods lived everywhere, in houses and hills, in streams and valleys, and in the sky. The roving stars were of great interest to the Greeks also, and they, too, assigned them to five of their greater gods—Hermes, Aphrodite, Ares, Zeus, and Kronos, later identified with their Roman equivalents.

Zeus was considered the father of the world and all things upon it. He was the god of thunder, of rain, wind, and dew—the spirit of the world. The mighty oak was the tree of Zeus. His brow was crowned with a wreath of olive leaves. In his right hand Zeus clutched a thunderbolt, and he held an ivory scepter topped with an eagle. His robes were purple spangled with gold. Offerings were made to Zeus by commanders of the army and rulers of the people.

Later in history, when the Romans became rulers of the world, they, too, had hundreds of gods. And chief among them was Jovis, whom they called Jupiter. To the Romans, Jovis was also the most important of the gods— the god of the sky, of rain and lightning. Temples to Jovis were built on hilltops, the appropriate location for the highest of the gods.

When Jovis was pleased, the god was a source of joy and happiness. The connection continues today in our use of the word "jovial" to describe a jolly person. And the English people have an expression "by Jove," which is a reminder of the ancient days when the Romans called upon this most important god to watch over them.

On a dark, moonless, and cloudless night, when the stars are bright and clear, you should be able to see Jupiter (or Marduk or Zeus or Jovis) just as people saw it thousands of years ago. It is a bright, starlike object that glows with a steady light—unlike the stars, which twinkle.

Like all the planets, Jupiter moves, constantly changing its position among the stars. You can find the location of Jupiter for any given time of the year in an almanac—or very often in a newspaper. Such articles on astronomy or "celestial events" will tell you whether Jupiter can be seen in the evening or in the morning, the constellation it is in, and often where it is in reference to the Moon—east, west, north, or south of it. Locating Jupiter may be easier if you keep in mind that it lies close to the path that the Sun travels across the sky.

REVOLUTION OF JUPITER

All the planets move around the Sun. Mercury, which is closest to the Sun, moves the fastest, and Pluto, which is usually the planet farthest from the Sun, moves slowest. The orbits of the planets are ellipses. You can draw an ellipse by standing two pins five or six centimeters apart in a piece of cardboard. Make a loop of string 10 or 12 centimeters long and drop it over the pins. Hold a pencil upright in the loop, with its point down, and draw a line, keeping the string taut on the pins. The resulting figure will be an ellipse. Each pin is a focus of the ellipse. In the solar system the Sun is one focus of the ellipse. When a planet is at the greatest distance from the Sun, it is at *aphelion* (*apo* is Greek for "away from" and *helios* for "sun"). When it is at the shortest distance from the Sun, it is at *perihelion* (*peri* is Greek for "near").

The mean distance of Pluto from the Sun is 5 911 million kilometers, whereas the mean distance of Neptune is 4 496 million kilometers. Consequently, we think of Neptune as being closer to the Sun than Pluto. However, when Pluto is closest to the Sun (perihelion), the distance is only 4 426 million kilometers. When Neptune is farthest from the Sun (aphelion), its distance is 4 507 million kilometers. When these two conditions coincide, as they do between 1979 and 1999, Neptune is actually farther from the Sun than Pluto.

Jupiter revolves extremely fast. Its day is only ten Earth hours long, and in view of the planet's enormous size, that is very fast indeed. But in traveling its orbit around the Sun, it is slower than Earth.

Earth moves almost 30 kilometers a second in its journey around the Sun—Jupiter travels 13 kilometers in a second. It takes us one year to make a complete journey around the Sun. It takes Jupiter 11.86 of our years to go once around. For Earth, one complete journey is some 950 million kilometers; a complete trip for Jupiter is close to 5 000 million kilometers.

When you look at Jupiter, you will not be aware of its motion. That's because it is so far away. Even though it is moving 13 kilometers a second, its position among the stars changes very slowly. It takes Jupiter a bit over six days to move a distance equal to the width of the full Moon. However, if you make a map of where Jupiter is among neighboring stars, and then check your map a week or two later, you'll be able to see that the position of Jupiter has changed, though not by very much.

MORNING AND EVENING "STARS"

Today people understand the differences between planets and stars. A star is a gaseous formation that produces energy. A planet does not produce energy. It is usually a relatively solid object that revolves around a star (although planets may also be largely gaseous). But there was no such clear understanding among the ancients.

To the people of Babylonia, all sky objects were stars of one kind or another. There were the long-haired stars (comets), shooting stars (meteors), new stars that suddenly shone brightly. Most of the stars did not move. But there were five that did. They moved among the other stars and so were called wanderers or *planetoi*—the Greek word for "wanderers." Occasionally even today planets are often called stars. For example when a planet was visible at sunrise, it was called a "morning star." When it could be seen in the early evening, it was called an "evening star." In books and reference tables you'll still see listings of both morning and evening "stars."

When Earth is on the same side of the Sun as Jupiter, we can see the planet in our night sky. When Earth is on one side of the Sun, and Jupiter is on the opposite side, the planet is in our daytime sky, and so we cannot see it. When Earth is at other locations in its orbit, we can see Jupiter either in our evening sky or just before sunrise.

RETROGRADE MOTION

Jupiter goes forward, and it appears to move backward. If you make a map and check the position of Jupiter over a period of several weeks, you'll probably notice that the planet is moving from west to east. This is the direction it actually follows in its journey around the Sun.

However, your map may indicate that the motion is directly opposite, from east to west. It would seem wrong, but you would be correct, for on occasion Jupiter does *appear* to move backward. It moves from west to east for thirty-nine weeks. Then it reverses its motion and moves from east to west for seventeen weeks. After this apparently "wrong" motion, the planet once again moves from west to east.

Other planets also have apparent forward-and-backward motions, forming "loops" and abrupt "reversals of direction" as they orbit. This activity was of great interest to the ancients. One of their main concerns was to explain how the planets were able to move in such a curious manner.

A complicated but quite acceptable explanation was developed by a Greek astronomer, Claudius Ptolemy, who lived in the second century of the Christian era. Ptolemy said that Earth was at the center of the universe and that the planets moved around it in circles. At the same time a planet moved in a smaller circle, the center of which was the epicenter. This epicenter was on the planet's orbit around Earth.

Ptolemy maintained that, when the planet was moving in the same direction as its epicenter (the center of its orbit), the planet moved forward (west to east). When the planet was moving on the other half of its journey around the epicenter, it appeared to be moving backward. (See the drawing on page 8.) This explanation of Ptolemy was accepted by most people for over a thousand years.

There were a few who believed the explanation was wrong, but their voices were not heard. Finally in 1543, a Polish astronomer named Nicholas Copernicus published another explanation for the forward-and-backward motions. Copernicus said that the Sun was the center of the universe and that all the planets—including Earth—rotated on their axes (thus seeing the Sun only during half of each one's "day") and at the same time revolved on orbits around the Sun. The backward-and-forward motions of the planets were only optical illusions, caused by changes in their positions relative to Earth.

The Earth moves faster than Jupiter, said Copernicus, so it catches up with the great planet and passes it. It is

PTOLEMY VIEW

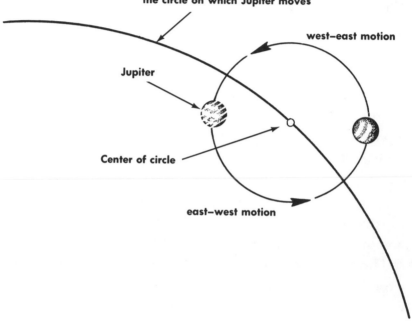

Path around Earth of the center of
the circle on which Jupiter moves

west–east motion

Jupiter

Center of circle

east–west motion

 Earth

Ptolemy system   According to early beliefs, the Sun and Moon orbited the
Earth, but the planets orbited the Sun. Therefore, at times a planet appeared to
move from west to east, and at other times from east to west.

when Earth passes Jupiter that Jupiter seems to be going backward. In a similar manner, when one train passes another on a neighboring track, the slower train seems (to the passengers on the faster train) to be going backward. The drawing on page 10 shows how our line of sight changes as Earth passes Jupiter.

Even though the Copernican view was reasonable, and it explained motions of the sky, many people argued against it. In their opinion the strongest argument was their own senses. Anyone could see that the stars, the planets, the Sun and Moon went around the Earth. They all rose in the east and set in the west; Earth was surely at the center of the universe. The argument went on for decades.

The Copernican idea got its greatest support some seventy years later, when the Italian astronomer Galileo Galilei looked into the sky through the newly invented telescope. He discovered four of Jupiter's satellites, bodies that went around Jupiter. And, Galileo said, this proved that all bodies did not move around Earth. Perhaps, after all, Copernicus was right when he said Earth is not the center of the universe.

GLOWING AND TWINKLING

When the night sky is clear of clouds and you are far from city lights, the stars stand out sharply. And, as you gaze at them, they appear to twinkle—to change in brightness. Planets, on the other hand, shine more steadily, appearing to glow. This is the chief visible difference between them when seen with the unaided eye: planets glow, and stars twinkle.

RETROGRADE LOOP

Against the stars Jupiter "appears" to move backward

Retrograde loop Jupiter always moves from west to east around the Sun. Earth catches up to Jupiter and passes it, causing the planet to appear to move backward.

Stars are very far away, much farther than planets—the nearest star is seven thousand times farther away than the farthest planet. Stars are so far from us that they appear to be points of light, even through the largest telescopes. The light beam does not pass freely through our atmosphere.

Our atmosphere is not the same throughout. Some parts are warmer than others; some parts contain more dust or water droplets than others. The single light beam from the star must pass through these different conditions of temperature, dust, and water droplets, so its passage is altered. These variations cause the light to change somewhat—the star twinkles.

Because planets are so much closer, they appear as disks and not as points. Therefore, a planet's light is made of several beams, each point on the disk producing a beam of light. These beams do twinkle; however, there are so many of them that the light evens out. We see the beams altogether as a single, glowing source. Look carefully after you've located Jupiter, and you'll probably see that it shines with a steady light, whereas the stars around it change in brightness—they twinkle.

BRIGHTNESS

Planets shine because they reflect sunlight. Therefore, you'd expect that those closest to us would be the brightest. And they would be if planets were all the same size and if their surfaces were alike. But the planets vary in size and in surface conditions.

Mercury has no atmosphere, so its surface is dull, dark, rocky material. It cannot reflect much light. In fact, Mercury is the poorest light reflector of all the planets, reflecting less than 1 percent of the light that falls on it.

Venus is the brightest of all the planets, sometimes reaching a magnitude of −4.4 (magnitude is explained below). It is covered with a whitish atmosphere that is a good reflector of light. Almost 60 percent of the sunlight that falls on the planet is reflected. (Earth reflects about 30 percent.)

Jupiter is also covered with an atmosphere, but there are many dark areas in it. Therefore, the planet cannot reflect as much light as Venus. About 44 percent of the sunlight that falls on Jupiter is reflected. Because Jupiter is very large, and because it is a good reflector, the planet often appears very bright. Some people say the light of Jupiter is bright enough to cause trees and buildings to cast shadows. Others dispute this claim. However, when Venus is at its brightest, trees and buildings do cast shadows. They are like the shadows you see on a moonlit night, though not as sharp or as dark.

The magnitude scale measures the brightness of stars. The ancient astronomers divided those stars they could see (without telescopes, of course) into six magnitudes, the first being the brightest and sixth magnitude the dimmest. Sirius, Canopus, and Alpha Centauri are stars of the first magnitude. There are some four to five thousand sixth-magnitude stars, many considered too unimportant to have names.

Today the concept of magnitude is still used. A star of the first magnitude is 100 times as bright as a star of the sixth magnitude. A star is said to be one magnitude higher (fainter) than another if it is dimmer by a ratio of 2.512.

Thus the *lower* the magnitude rating, the *brighter* the star. The Sun has a magnitude of −26.7. The full Moon has a magnitude of −12.

With the invention of the telescope it was found that there are many millions of stars dimmer than sixth magnitude. In fact, the dimmest star that can be photographed by the 200-inch telescope on Mount Palomar is +23. That's 6 250 000 times dimmer than a sixth-magnitude star.

PLANET	GREATEST MAGNITUDE
Mercury	−1.9
Venus	−4.4
Mars	−2.8
Jupiter	−2.5
Saturn	−0.4
Uranus	+5.7
Pluto	+12.0

CHAPTER 2

THE VOYAGER MISSIONS

The earliest planets explored by spacecraft were those closest to the Earth—Venus, Mercury, and Mars. Each of these is a terrestrial planet, so called because it has a high density not unlike that of Earth.

The mean density of Earth is 5.52, meaning that if one were to take a cupful of mixture of the rock, soil, and water, it would weigh 5.52 times the weight of an equal volume of water. The terrestrial planets have the following densities: Mercury 5.50; Venus 5.23; and Mars 3.93.

The other planets have much lower densities:

PLANET	DENSITY (water = 1)
Jupiter	1.33
Saturn	0.69
Uranus	1.56
Neptune	1.54
Pluto	0.80 (?)

The low-density planets are called the gaseous planets. We've never been able to see any solid surfaces—perhaps they don't exist, or if they do, they are small. Notice that Saturn and Pluto have densities that are lower than the density of water—that is, lighter than an equal volume of water. Thus, if there were an ocean gigantic enough to hold them, they would float.

Scientists were delighted with the information they had gathered about the terrestrial planets, but they were anxious to explore a gaseous planet. In the early 1970's two unmanned spacecraft called Pioneers 10 and 11 made the long journey to Jupiter. It was feared that spacecraft leaving the "inner" part of the solar system might be shattered by collisions with asteroids—a belt of rocky material circling the Sun in an orbit between those of Mars and Jupiter. The fear was reasonable because there are thousands of asteroids, and some of these chunks of rock and metal are several hundred kilometers across. Fortunately neither of the Pioneers had serious collisions, although there were many encounters with smaller particles.

The Pioneer probes sent back a tremendous amount of information. Pioneer 10, which passed within 130 000 kilometers of Jupiter on December 3, 1973, took spectacular color photographs of the giant planet, measured its temperature, confirmed the presence of helium, and discovered that the satellite Io has an ionosphere. Pioneer 11 confirmed much that Pioneer 10 had revealed and then went on to gather valuable information about Saturn. Eventually they became the first man-made objects to leave the solar system.

In the summer of 1977, two additional craft were launched, Voyagers 1 and 2. They were carried into space

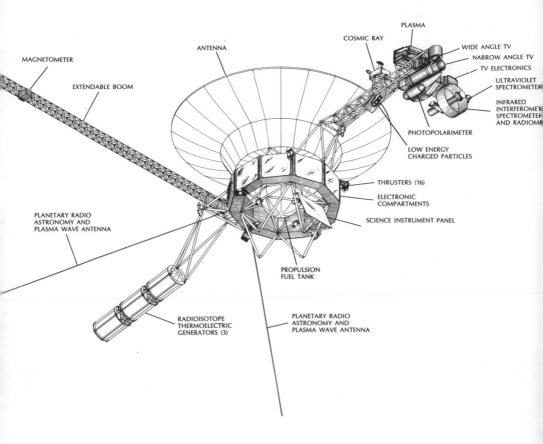

MAGNETOMETER

EXTENDABLE BOOM

ANTENNA

COSMIC RAY

PLASMA

WIDE ANGLE TV

NARROW ANGLE TV

TV ELECTRONICS

ULTRAVIOLET SPECTROMETER

INFRARED INTERFEROMET SPECTROMETE AND RADIOM

PHOTOPOLARIMETER

LOW ENERGY CHARGED PARTICLES

PLANETARY RADIO ASTRONOMY AND PLASMA WAVE ANTENNA

THRUSTERS (16)

ELECTRONIC COMPARTMENTS

SCIENCE INSTRUMENT PANEL

PROPULSION FUEL TANK

RADIOISOTOPE THERMOELECTRIC GENERATORS (3)

PLANETARY RADIO ASTRONOMY AND PLASMA WAVE ANTENNA

The Voyagers are planet probes that are loaded with a variety of instruments for gathering information about Jupiter and its satellites. Radios aboard the probes sent the information to receivers located on Earth.

by Titan/Centaur rockets, launched from Cape Canaveral, Florida—Voyager 1 sixteen days after Voyager 2. Since the path of Voyager 1 was more direct than that of Voyager 2, it arrived at Jupiter four months ahead of its twin—March 5, 1979.

Voyager 2 was aimed on a course that would eventually carry it past Uranus and Neptune, but after Jupiter, Voyager 1 would visit only Saturn. So, their courses were not the same. During the voyages, signals from Earth tested the instruments and also turned on devices that measured the particles in interplanetary space. Electric power for the instruments was generated by nuclear reactors. Spacecraft that had explored the inner part of the solar system had used solar cells to generate electricity. They could do so because the craft were close enough to the Sun to receive intense sunlight. The Voyagers (like the Pioneers before them), could not rely on sunlight, for intensity drops off rapidly as distance increases. Thus the surface of Jupiter receives only 1/27th as much solar energy as does Earth's surface.

Jupiter probes had to generate their own electricity. To do this they were equipped with devices called radioisotope thermoelectric generators. Radioactive particles produced heat which in turn was used to generate electricity. The reactors were located on arms that extended some distance from the spacecraft. This was done to prevent radiation from interfering with the operation of the instruments.

Detailed photographs from this space vehicle revealed great turbulence in the atmosphere of Jupiter and astonishing diversity among the satellites Io, Ganymede, Europa, and Callisto—called the Galilean moons, because they were first discovered by Galileo. Voyager 1 also revealed that Jupiter had rings much like those of Saturn. Composed of a quantity of particles, Jupiter's rings encircled the planet in a belt 9 000 kilometers wide and 30 kilometers thick, 58 000 kilometers above the planet's atmosphere.

But most surprising of all, photographs from Voyager 1 revealed that Io, the innermost satellite of Jupiter, contains live volcanoes. The space vehicle actually photographed one in the course of eruption. This indicates that Io, like Earth, is still changing—as far as we have proof, the only other active world in the solar system.

Voyager 2, which flew past Jupiter on July 9, took pictures that confirmed and further refined the information relayed by Voyager 1. Io's "first" volcano was no longer erupting, but several others were spotted, and Europa was seen to be smooth and covered by ice.

The Voyagers, which are still sailing through space, are the fastest objects ever to have been launched from Earth. At speeds of some 40 000 kilometers an hour, they crossed the Moon's orbit after only ten hours. (Apollo vehicles took about three days to reach the Moon.) Also, the Voyager missions marked the end of direct launching of spacecraft. Hereafter satellites, space probes, and planetary missions will be launched from shuttle orbiters.

Both of the Voyagers faced hazards at launching and throughout the flights. But Voyager 1 was the most imperiled, for it was deliberately aimed to within 300 000 kilometers of Jupiter to get a close-in view of Io, the innermost of the Galilean satellites. This is the region where radiation particles are concentrated most densely. Voyager 2 was much farther out (over 600 000 kilometers), even beyond the orbit of Europa, when it made the closest approach to Jupiter. The risk of sending Voyager 1 through the intense radiation area was high. The particles there

Voyager 1 passes through the flux tube of Io, a region of magnetic and plasma interaction between Io and Jupiter.

are so energetic there was a good chance that instruments would be destroyed and communication with the craft lost. Fortunately, the Voyagers made the pass safely.

Radio communication with the spacecraft—signals to them and information from them—was by giant antennas, that is, radio telescopes. These were located in California, Spain, and Australia. They were 120 degrees apart, all around the world, to ensure that one or the other location would always be in contact with the space-craft as the Earth rotated. However, contact was not instantaneous, as it is here on Earth.

When Voyager 1 flew past Jupiter it took 37 minutes for radio signals to reach Earth. By the time Voyager 2 reached Jupiter, the planet had moved farther from Earth, and so it took 52 minutes for the signals to reach us. If any malfunction had developed, or even if the Voyager had been demolished, ground control would not have known about it until almost an hour later.

During their flights the Voyagers radioed 30 000 photographs back to Earth. They were sent in computer language by a tiny 3-watt transmitter. (A moderate-sized electric bulb is 60 watts.) The pictures were taken with television-type cameras. Each picture was composed of 640 000 dots, which were converted to computer language before they were radioed to Earth.

When the signals were picked up by the Earth-based antennas, they were relayed to a processing center. There the signals were changed to dots by a computer and assembled to produce the original pictures. Small light dots created an image of light areas. Larger, heavier dots indicated dark areas. (If you look at any news photo through a magnifying glass, you will see that it, too, is made up of dots.) Color pictures were made of three images, each taken through a colored filter—blue, orange, and green. Computers combined the pictures and thus reproduced the original color. When needed to enhance a picture, one color could be emphasized over another. In this way, certain details stand out more sharply, and so scientists are able to see them more clearly.

The photographs of Jupiter and its satellites are dramatic, and they provide much thrilling new knowledge about the giant planet. Equally exciting was the information obtained by other instruments aboard the Voyagers and the earlier Pioneers: a meteoroid counter to record the number of collisions with particles in space; an infrared radiometer to measure heat given off by Jupiter and locate "hot spots" in the cloud layers; an ultraviolet photometer to determine the amount of hydrogen and helium in the atmosphere. It was possible to detect these gases because certain wavelengths of solar ultraviolet light are reflected by them, and those wavelengths were picked up by the instrument.

Another instrument was designed to measure radiation particles given off by Jupiter. This instrument, together with a cosmic-ray detector, enabled scientists to map the powerful radiation belts that surround the planet.

The instruments aboard the spacecraft worked perfectly, even better than the designers thought they would. They provided so much information that it will take years to evaluate it. But whenever discoveries are made, new problems arise. The Voyagers were no exception to this rule. Now scientists have additional questions about the planet. We'll discuss some of them after we consider what is known about Jupiter.

CHAPTER 3

THE GIANT PLANET

Jupiter represented the chief god of the Babylonians, the Greeks, and the Romans. And it is certainly the "king" among the planets. It is so large that 1300 Earths could fit inside it. The planet is made up primarily of ices and gases. The mass of Jupiter (the amount of material it contains) is 318 times the mass of Earth. In fact, Jupiter contains more than twice the material in all the other planets put together.

The diameter of Jupiter across the equator is 142 900 kilometers. By comparison, the equatorial diameter of Earth is 12 757 kilometers. The diameter of Jupiter is slightly more than 11 times greater. A journey around the Earth is a bit over 40 000 kilometers; a trip around Jupiter is almost 450 000 kilometers.

Jupiter is indeed the giant of the solar system; its diameter is 11 times that of
Earth. In this striking photograph, Io can be seen in front of Jupiter, with Europa
to the right.

ATMOSPHERE

Jupiter is a huge ball of gases and liquids, probably with no solid core of rocky metallic material such as that of Earth. The only part of Jupiter that is visible is the outer part of the atmosphere, and so our knowledge of the total atmosphere is limited. However, we'll learn more in the late 1980's when Galileo, the name of a planet probe we'll discuss later, will shoot new instruments deep inside Jupiter's atmosphere.

At the surface we can see dark and light belts that run all around the planet. The lighter regions appear to be higher than the dark belts. It has been suggested that the light areas are made of warmer gases that rise rapidly, cool, and then fall back into the planet. The darker belts are the more or less quiet zones between these rapidly rising gases. They blow both east and west. And all are sped along by the rotation of the planet—at about some 45 000 kilometers per hour. (Earth rotates about 1 680 kilometers per hour.)

Here and there one sees small, lighter patches in the dark bands. Close-up pictures taken with cameras aboard planet probes show that the patches are storm centers. They are tremendous masses of swirling gases, often as large as Earth, or larger. These gases race around at speeds up to two or three hundred kilometers an hour.

The most impressive swirl was first seen more than a hundred years ago, and it still exists. It is called the Great Red Spot, and it is so large that two Earths could be placed side by side inside it.

The large picture at right shows the great variety of

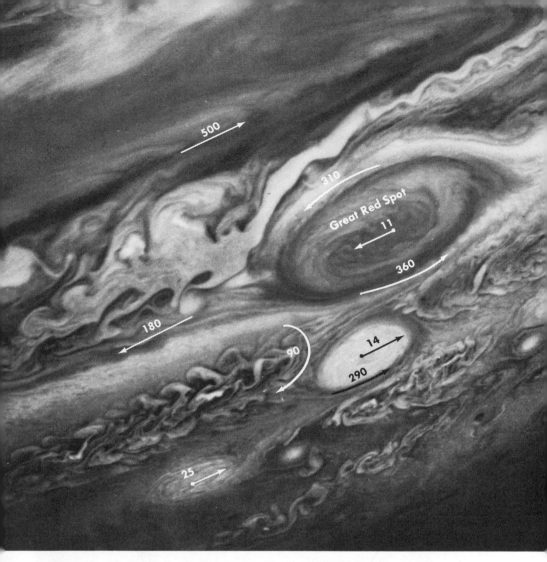

Jupiter's atmosphere contains "cells" (such as the Great Red Spot shown here), around which winds blow, some at high velocities. The cells themselves drift in many directions.

movements of the gases, some traveling slowly, 10–12 kilometers an hour, and others 300–500 kilometers an hour. The patches, or cells, may be very much like hurricanes that develop in Earth's atmosphere. But unlike Earth's storms, which last only a few days, those on Jupiter may continue for years—or even centuries. They can do so because there is no surface; Jupiter has no irregularities. Here on Earth storms break up because of variations in the surface—mountains, valleys, oceans, plains, cold and hot regions. Also, large cities interrupt the flow of the wind.

Our atmosphere is made up for the most part of nitrogen and oxygen. The atmosphere of Jupiter is mainly hydrogen and helium. All of the gases that compose its atmosphere are invisible. We see dark and light bands because clouds of various materials have formed: ammonia crystals (frozen ammonia), which are made of nitrogen and hydrogen; crystals of ammonium hydrosulfide (nitrogen and hydrogen plus oxygen and sulfur); also frozen methane, a mixture of carbon and hydrogen. It seems there are also crystals of frozen water at lower levels.

The swirling mixture of these outer materials is probably only a hundred kilometers deep, compressed by the planet's surface gravity—2.64 times that of Earth. Underneath this relatively thin atmosphere lie massive quantities of hydrogen and helium. These gases mix together and very likely form layers or shells, tens of thousands of kilometers thick, around a small core of liquid gases.

The clouds and deep layers of gases are pulled downward toward the center of the planet. As they pack closer together, temperature goes up. It probably reaches 30 000 degrees Celsius, which is about five times hotter than the surface of the Sun.

Near the center of the planet, pressure is very high, some say a hundred million times the pressure at Earth's surface. When pressure is so high, gases become metallic

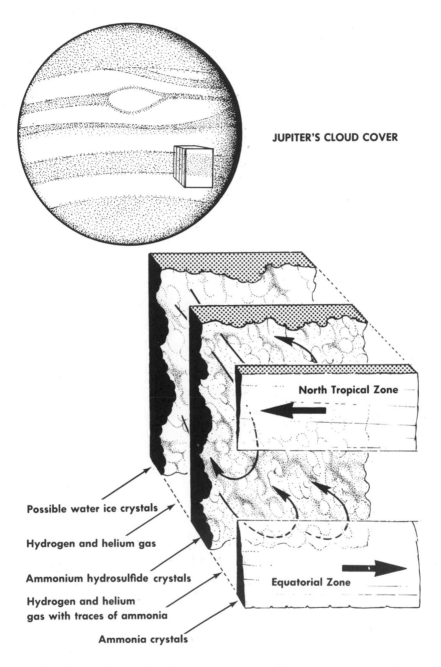

JUPITER'S CLOUD COVER

North Tropical Zone

Equatorial Zone

Possible water ice crystals

Hydrogen and helium gas

Ammonium hydrosulfide crystals

Hydrogen and helium
gas with traces of ammonia

Ammonia crystals

Layers of atmosphere The atmosphere of Jupiter appears to be made of layers,
with water crystals below layers of hydrogen, helium, and crystals of ammonia.

liquids, able to conduct electricity. The high temperature agitates this liquid, so that its movements produce a great magnetic field, extending out from the planet for 7 million kilometers.

MAGNETOSPHERE

Earth also has a magnetic field—that is, it behaves like a huge magnet. Its ends or poles, the points at which the force is concentrated, are located at the North and South Magnetic Poles. The Magnetic Poles are not identical with the North and South Poles (latitudes 90 degrees north and south), around which the Earth rotates. Instead the North Magnetic Pole is now believed to lie at a latitude 76.2 degrees north and longitude 101 degrees west, at Bathurst Island, Canada. The South Magnetic Pole is located at latitude 66 degrees south and longitude 139.1 east, in the South Pacific Ocean.

The force of this huge Earth magnet extends out to about 100 000 kilometers beyond the Earth's surface. And this region, within which the magnetism is measurable, is called the magnetosphere.

Jupiter's magnetosphere is not only much larger than Earth's but exerts tremendous force—about twenty times greater than Earth's. If one could see the magnetosphere, it would look something like a comet, its head being toward the Sun and its tail pointing away from it.

The magnetosphere is not only a region of magnetic force. It is also a region that contains ions of hydrogen, oxygen, and sulfur. (Ions are atoms that have been stripped of some of their electrons.) The ions are pushed

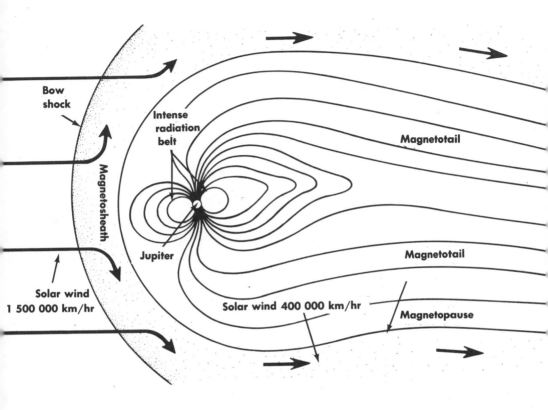

Bow shock

Intense radiation belt

Magnetosheath

Magnetotail

Jupiter

Magnetotail

Solar wind 1 500 000 km/hr

Solar wind 400 000 km/hr

Magnetopause

Magnetosphere   Jupiter is surrounded by a magnetic field, the magnetosphere. Particles in the solar wind push against the magnetosphere, flattening it on the Sun side, and causing it to trail far beyond the planet on the side away from the Sun. Inside the magnetosphere, belts of powerful radiation particles lie closer to the planet.

together toward Jupiter by the solar wind. This is a stream of protons and other atomic particles that speed away from the Sun at 1.5 million kilometers an hour. These particles bombard those in the magnetosphere and produce radiation belts around Jupiter. The particles in the belts contain tremendous amounts of energy, so much that humans could not penetrate them without being exposed to deadly radiation. It appears that no spaceship with people aboard will ever be able to move close to the great planet, although unmanned probes have done so without any noticeable damage.

Occasionally high-energy particles are ejected out into space, and these cosmic particles often have enough energy to reach as far as Mercury. A good many of the particles are trapped by our own planet. People used to think that all cosmic particles that bombard Earth came from outside the solar system. Today it is believed that a good number of them originate in the radiation belts of Jupiter.

AURORAS ON EARTH AND ON JUPITER

Earth is also surrounded by radiation belts that surround us. It is as though our planet were in the hole of a doughnut. Within the doughnut, electrons speed back and forth, from north to south.

Occasionally the belts become overloaded, and electrons spill out. They are pulled toward the polar regions. Some one hundred kilometers above the surface, the electrons collide with particles in our atmosphere. These collisions excite the atoms in those particles, causing them to give off visible light, the color depending upon the kind of atom involved in the collisions. A display of these colored lights produces our auroras—the northern lights, or aurora borealis, as they are called in the Northern Hemisphere, and southern lights, or aurora australis, in the Southern.

Auroras also occur on Jupiter, but they are probably not caused by the same phenomena. Instead, scientists believe, the Jovian auroras are caused by electric charges that flow between Jupiter and a region surrounding the path of Io, one of Jupiter's satellites. The orbit of Io seems to be inside an invisible tube (or tire shape) of highly charged electrified particles. A powerful electric current apparently flows from the polar regions of Jupiter and through this charged region to Io and back again. Jovian auroras are produced as this current collides with hydrogen and helium particles in Jupiter's atmosphere.

ALMOST A STAR

A star is a mass of gases in which nuclear reactions are occurring. It generates energy of many kinds—heat, radio waves, X rays, ultraviolet rays—and it shines because of the light it produces.

When a star is in the process of forming, tremendous amounts of hydrogen, helium, and other gases pack together. As gravity pulls in more and more gases, temperature goes up and up. When there are enough gases and when these gases are packed together tightly enough, temperature in the interior may reach 10 million degrees.

At that point, gases are hot enough to start nuclear reactions, and they become a star. The nuclei (cores) of hydrogen atoms join together to make helium. In the process, heat and other forms of energy are released, and the heat is radiated into space.

The planets are leftovers. They are made of materials that were left after stars had formed. The Sun contains 99.86 percent of the mass (quantity of material) in the solar system, which means that the planets and their satellites together add up to much less than 1 percent. Of that less than 1 percent, most is in Jupiter.

Hydrogen and helium make up most of the mass of Jupiter. And they also make up most of the mass of the Sun. However, other substances are also present—materials such as sulfur, oxygen, carbon, and nitrogen.

When Earth was formed, it probably contained large amounts of hydrogen and helium, too. But Earth did not have enough gravitation to hold the gases, so they escaped.

Jupiter had enough gravity to hold on to the gases, and still holds them. When the planet was formed, the gases packed close together, and so heat was generated—but not enough heat to start nuclear reactions. So Jupiter never became a star. Since that time, the giant planet has been cooling. And it is still losing heat that was generated at the time the planet was formed.

A planet such as ours gives off as much heat as it receives from the Sun, so the temperature of the Earth as a whole remains even. Jupiter is different. It gives off much more heat than it receives. The extra heat probably comes from the heat that developed when Jupiter first formed, thus the great planet is releasing heat that is billions of years old. Heat may also be generated by contraction of the planet. Jupiter is believed to have shrunk from a diameter of 200 000 kilometers to its present 143 000 kilometers and may still be shrinking.

If Jupiter had about ten times the mass it actually possesses, it would have had enough for the temperature to reach 10 million degrees. It would have become a star. But even though it is not massive enough to be a star, Jupiter has enough mass—and gravitation—to hold a system of more than a dozen satellites. Most of these are very tiny, with diameters of only a few kilometers. But three of them are larger than our Moon.

THE RINGS OF JUPITER

In 1610 Galileo looked through his low-power telescope at Saturn (see page 35). He noticed what appeared to be bulges on either side of the planet. Not knowing what they were, Galileo said that "Saturn has ears." He had discovered the rings of Saturn.

In the following years telescopes were improved, and astronomers were able to see the rings more clearly. They discovered that there were several rings with separations between them. Also, the ring system is wide, 273 000 kilometers in diameter, and perhaps only 50 or so kilometers thick. For the most part, the rings seem to be made of small ice particles.

As far as anyone knew, Saturn's rings were unique. For 367 years everyone believed that no other planet had rings. Then astronomers discovered that there was another ringed planet.

The group was in an airplane that carried a large telescope, flying high enough to get out of Earth's dense atmosphere. In order to gather information about the atmosphere of Uranus, they were going to watch that planet move in front of a star. However, about thirty-five minutes before Uranus reached the star, the star nearly flickered out. It did this five times before the planet itself moved in front of the star. Then it nearly flickered out five more times after Uranus had passed it. The watchers had discovered that Uranus has five rings.

Later on the investigators found there were four more rings, though extremely dim ones. These rings seem to consist of small pieces of rocky material twice as dark as Earth's satellite. And the formations are very thin, perhaps not more than five kilometers.

The discovery of the rings of Uranus suggested to some scientists that Voyager should look for rings around Jupiter. Many others were convinced there were no rings around the giant planet, and felt it was a waste of time and money even to look for them. However, the pro-ring group won out.

When Voyager 1 moved close to Jupiter, it discovered there was a ring system. Voyager 2, which followed about four months later, photographed the rings. There seem to be at least three of them. The brightest is about 800 kilometers wide. It appears to be made of rocky particles, most of them a fraction of a centimeter across, with larger particles scattered throughout the others.

It has been suggested that, unlike the rings of Saturn and Uranus, the rings of Jupiter are made of particles that do not stay in orbit, but compose the rings momentarily as the particles are passing through to the planet. Jupiter has

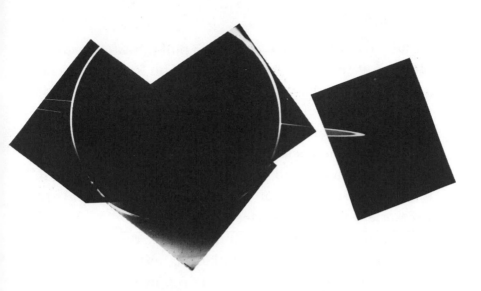

Jupiter, Saturn, and Uranus have rings as well as satellites. The rings of Jupiter are shown here in a combination of three different photographs.

a powerful gravitation pull, and the particles may be debris that the planet sweeps up as it moves around the Sun. Another theory is that the particles may be debris that is thrown out by the volcanoes of Io. They are trapped momentarily in the region of the rings but finally are pulled into the planet itself.

Four of the planets of the solar system are gaseous giants. Rings have been found around three of them—Saturn, Uranus, and Jupiter. Astronomers think it is likely that Neptune also has rings, though no sign of them has been detected as yet.

Many theories explain why a planet has rings. One of them refers to what is called the Roche limit. In 1850 Edouard Roche, a French scientist, suggested that if a satellite moves too close to a planet, the planet's gravitational force will be great enough to pull the satellite apart, reducing it to small bits and pieces. The Roche limit, beyond which a satellite is safe from such destruction, is 2.44 times the radius of the planet. This is measured from the center of the planet to the center of the satellite.

Perhaps some ancient moon veered too close to Jupiter and disintegrated, and it is the crumbs and fragments of this former satellite that are held in a ring around the equatorial region of the great planet.

But astronomers will continue to study the rings of Jupiter and those of the other planets, and they will continue to search for rings around Neptune. Perhaps one day they will learn what causes them.

CHAPTER 4

JUPITER'S SATELLITES

The Moon is our satellite. It moves around Earth, and it is controlled by Earth's gravitation. Until the early 1600's no one knew that there were any other satellites in the solar system.

Then early in January 1610, Galileo looked at the heavens through a telescope (the first man to do so). The year before, he had heard of a marvelous "optik tube" that had recently been invented in the Netherlands. Understanding the principle behind it, Galileo built his own telescope. In fact, he made dozens of them. The best was about equal to a small, inexpensive telescope available today in a variety store. But crude or not, what it showed him revolutionized astronomy.

When Galileo first looked at Jupiter, he was able to see three dim, starlike dots. One was west of Jupiter and two were east of the planet. The next night all three were west of Jupiter. As Galileo continued to gaze at the great planet, he discovered that there was another object that

Photographs of the four Galilean satellites of Jupiter, taken by Voyager 1. Clockwise from top left: Io, Europa, Callisto, and Ganymede.

changed positions, making a total of four. As a believer in the solar system of Copernicus, he decided that Jupiter had satellites that moved around it in the same manner that Venus and Mercury moved around the Sun.

These four satellites are now called the Galilean satellites in honor of their discoverer. In order of their distance from Jupiter, they are Io, Europa, Ganymede, and Callisto—all names of mythological creatures associated with the Roman god Jupiter.

You can see the satellites just as Galileo saw them. Some people say they can even see the four with their unaided eyes, although most people certainly cannot. You need a telescope, though not a very powerful one, or a pair of binoculars. (When you use binoculars, however, they should be braced. Otherwise your body motions make the image move, and seeing becomes difficult. Get a clamp and fasten the binoculars to something solid, a chair back, fence rail, or some such support.)

Once you locate the satellites, make a drawing of their positions. A night or two later, put their new positions on your drawing. You will see that the satellites go around Jupiter just as Galileo said they did over 350 years ago. As you continue to observe the satellites, if may be helpful to know the times required for them to go around Jupiter.

SATELLITE	TIME TO MAKE ONE REVOLUTION	
	DAYS	HOURS
Io	1	18
Europa	3	13
Ganymede	7	3
Callisto	16	16

Galileo's discovery caused a sensation. Before then, although many learned men had accepted Copernicus' theory of the solar system, there had been no way to prove it. People believed what they could see—and they "saw" that the Sun encircled the Earth and that there were five planets "wandering" among the stars, which apparently were also going around Earth. When Galileo reported that Jupiter had moons, he proved that Copernicus was right—all objects did not move around Earth.

Thus the discovery of Io, Europa, Ganymede, and Callisto was the first proof that the Ptolemaic system was incorrect. Gradually men began to change their minds and swing over to belief in a Sun-centered universe.

THE SPEED OF LIGHT

Later in that same century, in 1675, Olaus Roemer, a Danish astronomer, used the Galilean satellites to make another exciting discovery.

At that time people did not realize that light could travel very fast from place to place. Some believed that light was everywhere and did not need to be explained. Some action took place in an area between you and a certain tree, for example, and that's why you could see it. The action and your seeing it happened in the same time frame.

Others, such as Roemer, believed that it took time for light (and the images it carried to your eyes and brain) to travel. But no way had been found to measure its speed. However, by observing and timing the movements of Io, Roemer was able to do so. He took note of the time when Io moved behind Jupiter and when it reappeared. He did this over and over again and found that Io moved behind Jupiter—or it was eclipsed—on an average of every 42½ hours. Sometimes the interval was shorter, and at other times it was longer.

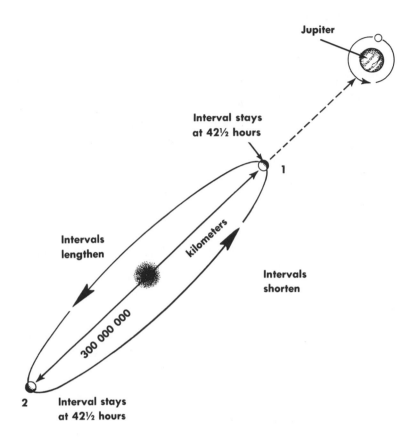

Jupiter

Interval stays
at 42½ hours

1

Intervals
lengthen

kilometers

Intervals
shorten

300 000 000

2   Interval stays
at 42½ hours

Roemer's experiment In 1625 Roemer noted that eclipses of Io occurred at intervals of 42 hours 30 minutes when Earth was at 1 and 2. As Earth moved
away from Jupiter, the intervals became longer. As Earth moved toward the
planet, they became shorter. One thousand seconds are required for light to
travel across the diameter of Earth's orbit.

In its journey around the Sun, Earth moves much faster than Jupiter, so Earth catches up and passes the great planet, and then the two are on the same side of the Sun. Then Earth moves away from Jupiter, and the planets are on opposite sides of the Sun.

Roemer found that, as Earth moved away from Jupiter, the eclipses of Io occurred at intervals greater than 42½ hours. As Earth moved toward Jupiter, the time between eclipses was shorter. When Earth moved neither toward nor away from the planet, Io was eclipsed exactly every 42½ hours.

The greatest increase in time between eclipses was close to 17 minutes, or 1000 seconds. Roemer said this was because the light from Io had to travel farther; it had to go across the entire diameter of Earth's orbit. At that time Earth's orbit was known to be 300 million kilometers. Since it took 1000 seconds for the light to travel 300 million kilometers, the light must travel 300 000 kilometers a second.

There were many who scoffed at Roemer and said the reasoning was ridiculous. Nothing could possibly travel so fast, they said. Later on, different methods were invented for finding the speed of light, and each came up with essentially the same answer, so Roemer was right. And that was way back in 1675.

When you are observing Jupiter's satellites, Io will be the one that appears closest to Jupiter. Other satellites are closer, but they are too dim to see easily. You'll be able to see Io pass behind Jupiter, just as Roemer did some three hundred years ago.

OTHER SATELLITES

In 1892—282 years after Galileo's discovery—another satellite of Jupiter was found. An American astronomer, E. E. Barnard, was the first to see it. He used a powerful 36-inch telescope to search the region close to Jupiter. The planet itself was very bright, so it was difficult to see objects close by. Nevertheless, Barnard was able to see a tiny speck of moving light, and he was able to see it on several occasions. It is now known as Amalthea, a potato-shaped satellite that is about 180 000 kilometers from the planet. This was the last satellite to be discovered by direct observation through a telescope. Since that time new satellites have been found by careful study of photographs.

Through the years astronomers found more satellites. Altogether, there appear to be sixteen satellites, and there may be many more. The names suggested for them are those of lesser gods of mythology. All of them are connected in some way to Jove (Jupiter) or to Zeus.

Usually the satellites are referred to by number. The Roman numbers in the list below give the order in which the satellites were discovered. The highest Roman number in the list is XIII, the satellite that was discovered in 1974. However, two more were discovered in 1979 and a third one in 1980, and they are presently called 1979 J-1, 1979 J-2, and 1980 J-3. They were discovered in pictures taken by Voyager. When other sightings of them are made, and the discovery is confirmed, these satellites will probably be numbered J-XIV and J-XV and J-XVI and be given appropriate names.

The sixteen satellites in order of their distance from Jupiter are these:

SATELLITES		DISTANCE FROM JUPITER in Thousands of Kilometers		DIAMETERS in Kilometers
1979 J-1	(J-XIV?)	57		50 (?)
1979 J-2	(J-XV?)	150		80 (?)
1980 J-3	(J-XVI?)	50 (?)		50 (?)
Amalthea	J-V	180		200 (?)
Io	J-I	422	The	3 640
Europa	J-II	670	Galilean	3 100
Ganymede	J-III	1 070	Satellites	5 270
Callisto	J-IV	1 855		4 990
Leda	J-XIII	11 094		10 (?)
Himalia	J-VI	11 470		150 (?)
Elara	J-VII	11 740		50 (?)
Lysithea	J-X	11 850		20 (?)
Ananke	J-XII	21 200		20 (?)
Carme	J-XI	22 560		20 (?)
Pasiphae	J-VIII	23 500		20 (?)
Sinope	J-IX	23 700		20 (?)

The four Galilean satellites are by far the largest of the satellites. The smaller moons that move in orbits between these four and Jupiter may be associated with the rings of Jupiter.

Far beyond the Galilean satellites, and extending 23 million kilometers, are the orbits of eight very small satellites. The four outermost may be asteroids that have been captured by the gravitational field of Jupiter. These four satellites move "backward," or retrograde—that is, opposite to the direction in which Jupiter rotates. All the other satellites move around Jupiter in the same direction as the planet itself rotates.

The four outer satellites are just close enough for Jupiter to hold on to them. Very likely, great numbers of asteroids have moved close to Jupiter. At the distance these four satellites are from Jupiter, however, they could not have been captured if they were moving in the same direction as the great planet. They would have been accelerated and thrown out into space. However, if an asteroid approached the planet moving opposite to Jupiter's rotation, it could have been captured, even at the great distance of those four outer satellites. Thus the four are probably captured asteroids. And since they are loosely held, they might eventually wander away from Jupiter.

But there are still plenty of other asteroids, and some of them may be captured by Jupiter, in which case they would be called satellites, and so over the years, the number of Jupiter's satellites may increase or decrease.

CHAPTER 5

IO, EUROPA, GANYMEDE, AND CALLISTO

Each of the Voyagers weighs about a ton and is loaded with cameras, power supplies, magnetic meters, and other instruments for gathering information and sending it back to Earth. Altogether we now have some 30 000 photographs of Jupiter and the four Galilean satellites. We'll look at a few of them and consider what they tell us about these distant worlds.

Io

In Greek mythology Io was a maiden who was loved by Zeus (Jupiter). To protect her from his wife's jealousy, Zeus turned Io into a heifer. Since all Jovian moons have been given names of mythological characters connected with the tales of Zeus, "Io" was picked as the name for the innermost of the Galilean satellites.

Io orbits Jupiter at some 422 000 kilometers. Perhaps

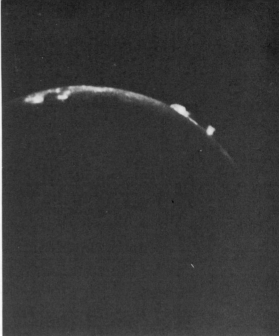

These photos show plumes from active volcanoes on Io. They prove that Io has the most active surface in the entire solar system.

the most exciting discovery about it—indeed, about any of the satellites—was made by Linda Morabito, a flight engineer at the Jet Propulsion Laboratory in Pasadena, California, who was a member of the Voyager team. While she was studying a photograph of Io made by Voyager 1, Linda looked more closely at the edge of the satellite. She saw an umbrella-shaped formation rising above the surface. It was an erupting volcano; debris from it was shooting 280 kilometers into space.

This was sensational news, for it was the first live volcano that had been seen anywhere in the solar system except on Earth. It meant that Io was an active world; it was growing and changing. It was a new world. By watching it, scientists hope to learn more about how our own planet came into existence.

Now that the team knew there was one volcano, they looked for more, and they found them. Eight volcanoes were found in the Voyager 1 pictures of Io. Four months later, when Voyager 2 went by, seven of the volcanoes were still erupting.

Since it is close to Jupiter, Io is pulled strongly toward the planet. At the same time Europa and Ganymede pull in the opposite direction. The two forces produce great bulges in the surface of Io; the surface goes up and down, up and down as much as a hundred meters every thirty-six hours. No doubt this motion is what makes the surface of Io so hot, in much the same way that a piece of wire gets hot when you bend it back and forth.

The surface of Io seems to have no craters made by collisions, such as those on Earth's Moon. But it is covered with dark and light spots, all of which may be the locations of volcanoes, either active or quiet. A large part of its surface crust is composed of sulfur and sulfur dioxide. In fact, sulfur is the main substance thrown out by Io's volcanoes. Below this, some scientists think, lies a double lithosphere—a sphere of rock within an outer sphere of rock. Layers of molten material are believed to alternate with them. According to this theory, Io consists of a core of molten silicate, surrounded by a rocky crust, which in turn is covered by a layer of molten sulfur and covered by a second rocky crust, plus its visible surface of sulfur.

Occasionally breaks occur in the surface of the satellite, and sulfur explodes through them. The rising and falling of the surface makes openings here and there, through which these explosions are released. Scattered over Io's surface are sulfur cones, the remains of volcanoes. They

CROSS SECTION OF IO

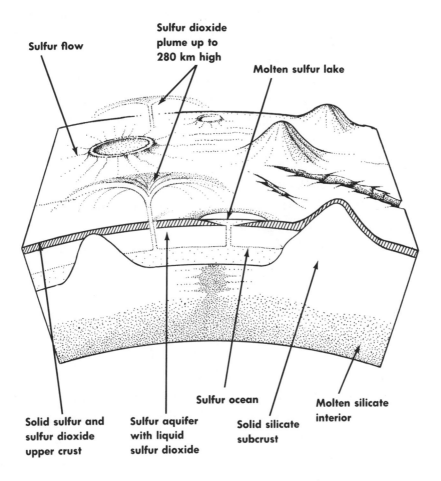

Sulfur flow

Sulfur dioxide plume up to 280 km high

Molten sulfur lake

Sulfur ocean

Molten silicate interior

Solid sulfur and sulfur dioxide upper crust

Sulfur aquifer with liquid sulfur dioxide

Solid silicate subcrust

Cross section of Io   The surface of Io may be covered with layers of sulfur. Beneath the surface there may be lakes and oceans of sulfur between formations of rock.

are surrounded by ridges of solid sulfur and rock, the "lava" of previous eruptions.

Io is large, a bit larger than the Moon, but it still does not have enough gravitation to hold an atmosphere. So there is no air on Io, nor is there any water. The sky around it is black, although there might be glowing areas—places where sodium vapor thrown out by volcanoes gives off light. The surface is probably covered by a thin layer of solid sulfur in mixtures of dirty black, yellow, and orange. Occasionally, however, there may be "snowfalls" of sulfur, and in the polar regions the sulfur snow may be several meters deep.

Light-colored patches of sulfur dioxide lie here and there, also, black lakes of solid sulfur, which formed as sulfur oozed onto the surface. The smell of Io is doubtlessly pretty bad.

The surface is apparently broken by wide holes, a kilometer deep and ten or so kilometers across. These are the cracks through which Io's volcanoes have exploded, tossing rock and sulfur skyward to arch over and crash to the surface. Occasional mountains rise as high as ten kilometers. But there are no collision craters on Io, so the satellite is probably the youngest body in the solar system. (It is believed that the more craters a body has—such as the Moon, Mars, and Mercury, for example—the older it is.)

Sulfur atoms and atoms of other materials are thrown into space and formed into a huge tire-shaped ring that surrounds the satellite. It is called the Io torus, and although it is invisible, the particles in it have electric charges. A powerful electric current flows through the torus and between Jupiter and Io.

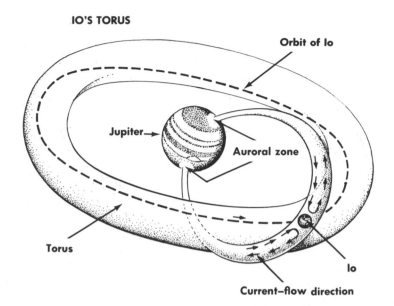

IO'S TORUS

Orbit of Io

Jupiter→

Auroral zone

Torus

Io

Current–flow direction

Io torus Io seems to be surrounded by an invisible tire-shaped cloud of charged particles called a torus. A powerful electric current apparently flows from Jupiter through the torus to Io. The current produces large, bright auroras in the atmosphere of Jupiter.

EUROPA

In Greek mythology, Europa was a maiden whom Zeus (Jupiter) approached after he had changed himself into a bull. Europa climbed on his back, and the two flew off to Crete.

Europa, a bit farther away from Jupiter than Io (670 900 kilometers), may be a young satellite, too. It is perhaps only 100 million years old, compared to Earth's 4.5 billion years. Certainly Europa contains very few craters. (It is believed that Europa has managed to "resurface" itself at some time in the past, but no one knows how.)

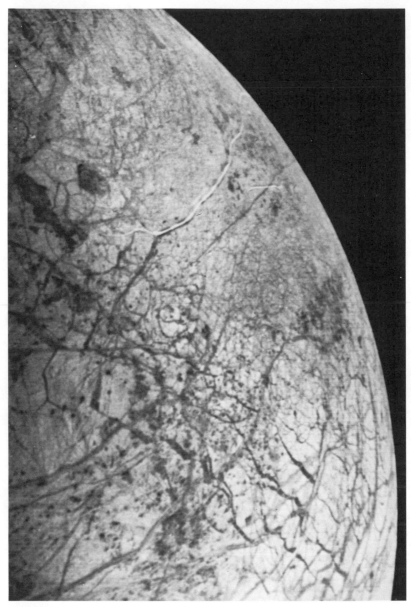

A thin layer of ice appears to cover the smooth surface of Europa. Beneath the ice there may be a slushy region some hundred kilometers deep. The dark streaks seem to be cracks that have been filled in, perhaps with ice and dust.

Europa is also the water satellite. Its smooth surface appears to be covered with ice. Photographs show that the planet is crisscrossed by dark lines, like the marks of skates on a frozen pond. These are probably cracks that have been filled in with ice and slush. Europa's surface is thought to be much like pack ice in Earth's Arctic regions.

Although the satellite's surface is smooth and cold, broken only by a few mounds of dirty ice, there is heat in its interior. This heat is probably created by the pull of the other satellites and of Jupiter itself. Occasionally the internal heat and pressure may push out geysers of water, which freeze into ice crystals and rain down on the surface.

GANYMEDE

In Greek mythology, Ganymede was the son of Tros, the king of Troy. He was carried away by Zeus (Jupiter), and became cupbearer to the gods. In Egypt he was given credit for causing the annual flooding of the Nile, which fed the crops.

Ganymede, 5 270 kilometers in diameter, is the largest of all the Galilean satellites. (Titan, a satellite of Saturn, with a diameter of 5 140 kilometers, is very nearly the same size.) Ganymede is also old, perhaps as old as our Moon. It has many craters, especially in dark areas.

Fifty percent of the satellite may be water, much of it in the form of ice. Over the millennia this thick ice surface—much thicker than Europa's—has been pounded into crushed ice by crashing meteorites.

A most curious feature of Ganymede is the large dark

A large, dark, heavily cratered region shows in this Voyager 2 photograph of Ganymede. The lighter areas are ridged and grooved sections that are younger than the dark area.

circular region. (Dark patches usually mean old regions, white and light mean young ones.) Light regions, such as the rays in the picture above, may be white because they are clear, clean ice. The darker regions are old, and they have accumulated dust and debris.

Curious parts of Ganymede are the areas where the surface is grooved and twisted, as though gigantic fingers had raked across it repeatedly, in every direction. There are troughs and ridges five to fifteen kilometers across, and new ones appear to lie above older ones. Very likely these

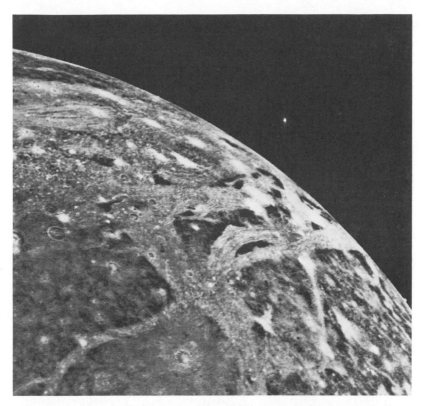

The surface of Ganymede appears to have been plastic enough to be pushed and squeezed, producing long ridges and valleys, often one atop the other.

are fracture marks. At one time huge pieces of Ganymede's crust broke away and moved about, piling into one another.

Scientists do not know why this happened, or how. Some believe that Jupiter pulled on Ganymede so strongly that it slowed down its spin. Now the satellite rotates around its axis at the same rate it revolves around Jupiter, so the same face of Ganymede is always toward Jupiter. (This is also true for the other Galilean satellites and for our own Moon.) While this slowdown was occurring, forces may have been great enough to cause the breakup of the surface into pieces, which then leveled and shifted.

In a similar fashion, the surface of Earth is broken into pieces (called tectonic plates) that lie on top of semimolten interior layers. These plates sometimes shift, grating against one another, thus causing earthquakes and volcano eruptions. Such disturbances most commonly occur at the edges of these huge sections. It is hoped that by studying Ganymede more closely, scientists will understand better the motion of Earth's own plates.

CALLISTO

In Greek mythology Callisto was a beautiful maiden who enticed Zeus (Jupiter) and so made his wife jealous. The goddess solved the problem by turning Callisto into a bear. To protect her from hunters, Zeus carried Callisto to the sky and placed her among the stars as the Great Bear (Big Dipper). Later her own name was borrowed for the fourth Galilean satellite of Jupiter.

Callisto is in many ways similar to Ganymede. It is old, and it is heavily cratered. In fact, Callisto is so covered with craters that in some sections they lie one on top of another. One crater—an immense dent called an impact basin—is 200 kilometers across. It must have been caused by collision with a gigantic meteoroid. The force and heat of this encounter probably melted part of the satellite's icy crust and allowed water to gush into the newly made hollow. This then froze again, forming a smooth surface.

The next chance you get, look at Jupiter, and keep

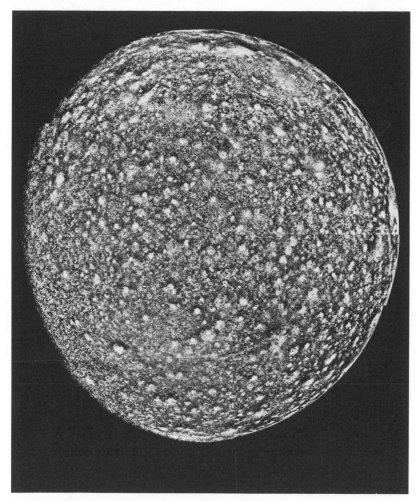

Callisto is the most heavily cratered object in the solar system, as can be seen from the hundreds of craters in this photograph. A very large one at one o'clock appears to have at least fifteen rings surrounding it. The limb (edge) of the satellite is smooth because of the icy composition.

watching the planet to see the changing positions of these four exciting satellites. With practice, and by watching over a period of several months, you'll be able to identify each one of them.

CHAPTER 6

LIFE ON JUPITER?

In 1969 and during the next few years, men walked on the Moon and explored the surface. One thing they were looking for was some sign of life. Not necessarily anything alive, but perhaps fossil remains of organisms that might have existed there at some time in the Moon's history. But no life was found, nor was there any sign of past life.

Probes explored Mercury and Venus, and instruments were landed on Mars. All of them were programmed to look for clues that would indicate the existence of life, either today or in the past. But no such clues were discovered. From all our explorations, scientists must conclude that Earth is the only place in the solar system where life is known to exist.

Jupiter may prove to be an exception, for this giant planet contains all the ingredients believed necessary for life to arise. In the late 1980's, scientists may find that simple organic molecules exist in Jupiter's atmosphere, and these could be the first stage in the development of organisms. If none are found, some scientists will still believe that such molecules may be created in the future as the atmosphere of Jupiter becomes less stormy.

The reason why some people think this might happen is because Jupiter's present-day atmosphere—ammonia, methane, water, and hydrogen—resembles that of Earth when it was first formed.

When the gases of Earth's atmosphere were exposed to energy discharges—heat from the sun, ultraviolet energy, or the energy in lightning flashes—amino acids were formed. Gradually these acids combined to make living cells. Scientists believe this because they have produced the same acids in laboratories. Methane, ammonia, and hydrogen were mixed with hot steam (water); an electric spark was discharged inside the mixture. When the steam was cooled, amino acids were found in the water.

In the early Earth, some of the amino acids probably drained out of the atmosphere into ancient seas. As more and more acids gathered in the seas, combinations of them eventually occurred. The amino acids then built themselves into primitive proteins—building blocks of living cells.

Energy is needed in the life-producing process. And there is not much solar energy on Jupiter—it is only 1/27th the intensity of that on Earth. But Jupiter has very powerful discharges of lightning, a billion times greater than lightning on Earth. It may be that, in the atmosphere of Jupiter, there are pockets of the four gases, and on occasion lightning may flash through them. Amino acids may form.

They may last for only brief periods because of the presence of other gases that interact with them or because of severe changes in temperature. However, Jupiter may eventually become a less violent planet. It may settle down enough for amino acids to remain intact—long enough to combine with other substances and produce protein. After millions of years, life of some kind may appear on Jupiter. And after millions of additional years, that life may become more and more complex, in much the way it did on our own planet.

CHAPTER 7

GALILEO SEEKS MORE ANSWERS

The Pioneers and Voyagers answered many questions about Jupiter, but there is much more to learn about the Jovian world. In 1986, after a three-and-a-half-year journey, a probe will continue our explorations—provided our government sets aside the money to pay for it. It will be parachuted into the atmosphere of Jupiter. The probe and the craft that will carry it to Jupiter are called Galileo, in honor of the Italian scientist.

It is hoped that the probe will give enough information about Jupiter's atmosphere so that we will know if the conditions are favorable for life to evolve. It is also hoped that it will provide clues to solving other mysteries.

Galileo will consist of three sections: an orbiter that will revolve around Jupiter, a probe that will be lowered into the atmosphere, and rocket engines that will transport them to the great planet.

The orbiter contains a radio, antennas, a power supply,

TV cameras, and various measuring instruments. The antenna is 5 meters across, and in many ways the orbiter resembles the earlier Voyagers.

The probe is cone-shaped, and inside it are measuring instruments and a radio transmitter. The outside of the cone is a shield for protection against the high temperatures that will be generated. There will also be great pressures, perhaps ten times that on Earth, so the probe must be designed to withstand them. The radio and instruments are powered by a battery, which is turned on when the probe moves into Jupiter's atmosphere.

At launch the orbiter is folded flat, the probe is fastened to it, and both are carried at the nose of rocket engines.

THE MISSION

Galileo will be carried into space in the cargo bay of a space shuttle. A shuttle is a vehicle that can fly cargo, laboratories, construction equipment—anything—into space, orbit with its cargo, and eventually return to Earth to be reused. One of the most important features of the new space-shuttle program will be more efficient exploration of space.

Once the shuttle is in Earth orbit, the cargo doors are opened, and Galileo is lifted out. It is put in line for a close approach to Mars. (The gravity of Mars will be used to accelerate Galileo and bend its path to one that will intercept Jupiter.) Three rocket engines fire in sequence, and Galileo leaves the shuttle behind as it begins its one thousand-day journey.

Five months before Galileo gets to Jupiter, the probe

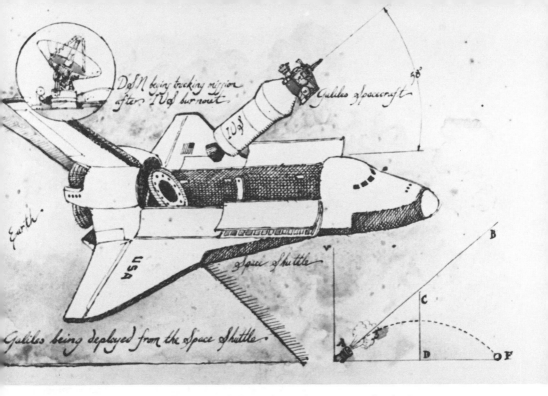

The Galileo space vehicle will be carried above the Earth in a space shuttle. From there it will be launched into a journey to Jupiter.

will be separated from the orbiter and put into its own flight path. If the probe goes in too steeply, frictional heating will change it to vapors. If the path is too flat, the probe will be deflected by the top layers of the atmosphere. Once the probe has been released, its path cannot be controlled, so the angle at release must be exactly correct.

With the probe on its way, the orbiter's rocket motor fires, putting it in a path that will place it above the atmosphere on the afternoon side of Jupiter. At that location, the orbiter will receive radio messages from the probe, and it will use its large antenna to retransmit the information to Earth.

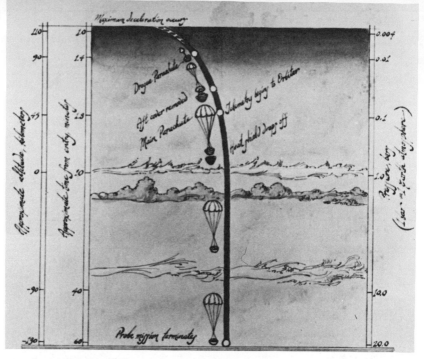

As the probe descends, a small (drogue) parachute slows it and removes the cover. The heat shield falls free, and a larger parachute slows descent through the atmosphere.

When the probe reaches Jupiter, it will be traveling 48 kilometers a second—172 800 kilometers per hour. On entering the atmosphere, it slows rapidly, so fast that the force is 400 times Earth's gravity. The heat shield glows white-hot. A small parachute opens and pulls away the rear cover of the probe. As this happens, a larger parachute opens, and the heat shield, which has cooled to a dull red, drops away.

Immediately, instruments start sending information about cloud layers, temperatures, and density to the orbiter, which is moving above the atmosphere. The signals continue for sixty minutes, until the probe enters a very high pressure layer. Then temperature again rises rapidly.

The high temperature and dense atmosphere will weaken the radio signal and finally cut it off completely.

At this time the orbiter rocket will burn for about fifty minutes to put it into a wide orbit around Jupiter. The orbit will take it close to Io. Then succeeding orbits will take it to each of the Galilean satellites. This survey will continue for twenty months. It will enable scientists to obtain close-up views of the satellites. Also, the orbiter will look at Jupiter and be able to observe changes that occur in the magnetosphere, plus the shifting of the Red Spot and other atmospheric cells.

PURPOSES

Galileo (the probe and the orbiter) is designed to give information about pressure, temperature, and density changes in Jupiter's atmosphere down to below the bottom layer of its water clouds. Very likely, the atmosphere is the original material of which the universe was composed, unchanged by the nuclear reactions that occur in stars. It may be the kind of atmosphere that Earth had when our planet first formed.

The energy balance of Jupiter is another area of investigation. How much solar heat penetrates into the atmosphere? How deep does it go? What is the source of heat given off by Jupiter? Is it heat left over from formation of the planet? Is it generated by contraction of the planet? Or is it caused by Jupiter's rapid rotation? What are the exact structure and composition of the cloud layers? How deep are they? What causes the reds, browns, and other colors that appear in the atmosphere?

Storms, often accompanied by tremendous lightning discharges, persist on Jupiter for months, years, even centuries. By watching closely the changes that occur in these storm systems, it is hoped we may better understand storms in our own atmosphere. If so, Galileo may help us find ways to predict weather more accurately, and perhaps even control it to some extent.

REGIONS OF THE MAGNETOSPHERE

Next to the Sun, Jupiter is the strongest source of radio signals in our sky. Since 1955 we have known that radio waves are associated with a magnetic field—the magnetosphere that surrounds the planet. For twenty months the orbiter will gather information about this tremendous area, and so day-to-day changes will be revealed. The magnetosphere appears to have three separate regions. The inner region is shaped like a doughnut; the planet is in the hole. This is much like Earth's magnetosphere. But the intensity of the particles in Jupiter's is much greater. Io, Europa, and Ganymede all move inside this region.

The middle region of the magnetosphere is made up of charged particles, whirled around by the magnetic field and by the rapid rotation of Jupiter—some 45 000 kilometers an hour.

The outer region separates the charged particles of the middle region from the electrons and protons that stream from the Sun in the solar wind. The area where these two forces meet is called the bow shock. The solar wind hits the magnetosphere here and presses it back toward the planet. Often the particles are deflected out into space again, and they speed across the solar system.

Volcanoes on Io probably supply high-speed ions of sodium, potassium, and sulfur to the magnetosphere. These are the particles that make the clouds around Io and the torus, or ring, that surrounds Jupiter. Studying these particles and how they change is important to understanding our own magnetosphere. Some believe that we may learn a lot about high-energy physics by observing the magnetosphere layers of Jupiter. Somewhere in this vast system there may be clues to finding ways to create and control fusion reactions—the ultimate solution to the world's energy dilemma.

The Galileo orbiter may remain active beyond twenty months, but ultimately its power generators will stop. The craft will become a solitary, silent wanderer, traveling around Jupiter but unable to give us any additional information.

CHAPTER 8

MESSAGES FOR ETERNITY

Spacecraft are designed to do certain jobs immediately after reaching their destinations. But designers have also fashioned many of them to make contact with future civilizations that may arise on our own planet, or with civilizations that may flourish among far-off stars, millions of light-years away.

Satellites placed high above Earth will remain in orbit long beyond our lifetimes and perhaps long beyond the time of modern man. For example, Lageos (for Laser Geodynamic Satellite) is expected to stay in orbit for 8 million years. It is a brass sphere that reflects laser beams sent from Earth. These reflected beams will measure slight movements of continents, or the tectonic plates of Earth's surface—motions as minute as two or three centimeters in a century.

In some distant time, Lageos may be recovered from orbit, or discovered where it may land on Earth. Two copies of a message from Earth are inside the satellite. They are 10-by-18-centimeter stainless-steel plaques.

At the upper left is the name and a drawing of the satellite. At the center are numbers from 1 to 10 in binary arithmetic—the simplest and most basic form of counting. At upper right, Earth is shown in orbit around the Sun, with an arrow indicating the direction of motion. The number 1 below Earth is for one revolution.

Below this are three drawings. The uppermost one shows Earth as it is believed to have been millions of years ago. The number beneath that drawing is the binary notation for about 250 million years. It is past time, as indicated by the arrow that points toward the left. (A left-pointing arrow is universally accepted as indicating past time.)

The middle map shows the world at zero time. The 0 has arrows pointing to both the past and the future, so the time is the present. The arrow indicates that Lageos was launched from the West Coast of the United States.

At the bottom, Earth is shown as geologists expect the continents will appear far in the future. Beneath it is a binary number that indicates roughly the time some 8 million years from now. (The right-facing arrow indicates the future.) No one can say what changes may occur in Earth's future. Creatures of all kinds may have disappeared. Certainly our civilization will have gone out of existence, and perhaps others will have developed. No matter who finds it, or when, the message aboard Lageos will be an intriguing puzzle. It is a postcard dispatched to the future, which will indicate some of our attempts to understand our own planet.

SPACE MESSENGERS

Messages to future civilizations were also considered by the designers of the Pioneer and Voyager satellites. These civilizations would not be on planet Earth, but rather at locations in deep space—far beyond the outer boundaries of the solar system. They would be somewhere among the 200 billion stars that compose our Galaxy.

Both the Pioneers and Voyagers are traveling in orbits that will eventually take them out of the solar system. Satellites in orbit around the Earth—Lageos, for example—are given a certain amount of energy, just enough to hold them in orbit. A spacecraft that goes to Venus, let us say, is pushed to a higher speed, because it must have enough energy to escape Earth's gravitational field. Once free of Earth, it is "captured" by the Sun's gravitational field and goes in toward the Sun until it approaches Venus.

The probes that went to Jupiter were given even larger boosts because they must escape into an outer orbit. As they neared Jupiter and flew past, the probes were accelerated by Jupiter's gravitation. This speeded them up enough to escape the sun's gravity and put them into orbit around the center of the Galaxy, where one orbit will take 250 million years.

PIONEERS

Pioneer 10, launched from Earth in 1972, will travel through space virtually forever. After passing the orbits of Pluto and Neptune, it will be in interstellar space—the space between the stars. It will be traveling 12 kilometers a second. Even so, it will take Pioneer 100,000 years to cover a distance equal to that of Proxima Centauri, the nearest star of the three-star system we call Alpha Centauri. However, the spacecraft is not going in that direction. It is heading out in the direction of the constellation Taurus and toward stars that are much farther away than Proxima Centauri. It may take Pioneer two million years to reach them.

When stars are created, they often form in pairs, one star traveling around the other. If they are not paired, then a single star may have lesser bodies moving around it, like our Sun and its family of planets. At the present we have no way of knowing whether there are planets in orbit around any other star. However, many investigators believe that planets, or systems of planets, may be usual. Solitary stars with no companion and no planets may be rare in the universe.

In our Galaxy there are some 200 billion stars. If only 1 percent of those stars have planets, this means there are 2 million planetary systems in this one section of the universe. The planets might be large and gaseous like Jupiter, but there may be others that are able to sustain life.

Pioneer (and Voyager, too) may never be seen by any living creature. The presence of Earth's messages may remain unknown forever, because there may be no one out beyond the solar system to receive them. But if there are planets of advanced civilization out there, they would doubtlessly be fascinated to find a spacecraft moving within range of their instruments. It is easy to imagine how it might be.

Engineers on those planets, or aboard their own space

vehicles, would see a strange blip on their radar screens. Curiosity would make them move in closer. After careful inspection the craft would be drawn into that alien ship and studied carefully. It would be a major curiosity.

Maybe it would be little more than that. The creatures might have little more intelligence than a fly, or they might have no awareness of the meaning of a picture. On the other hand, the creatures might have a culture and civilization that far exceed ours, and so they might look upon the spacecraft as a crude product of a primitive society.

In their perusal of the Pioneer craft this alien society we have imagined would come across a gold-plated aluminum plaque. Perhaps some among them would study it and figure out the meaning of its symbols. They carry information about the Earth-based civilization that launched the craft. The information is in the sciences, for it is believed that basic science is universal. Gravity, electricity, molecular structure, magnetism, radiation—such forces and conditions are no different on Proxima Centauri from those same things on Earth. Science, the universal knowledge, would seem to be the way to communicate with an alien civilization, in place of local concerns such as language, religion, politics, and history.

Hydrogen is the most common element in the universe. It is the base from which the other elements were made at the time the universe came into being. Therefore, hydrogen is represented at the upper left of the plaque, along with its change from one energy state to another. Just below, the locations of Earth and the Sun are shown with respect to fourteen pulsars (sources of interstellar radio

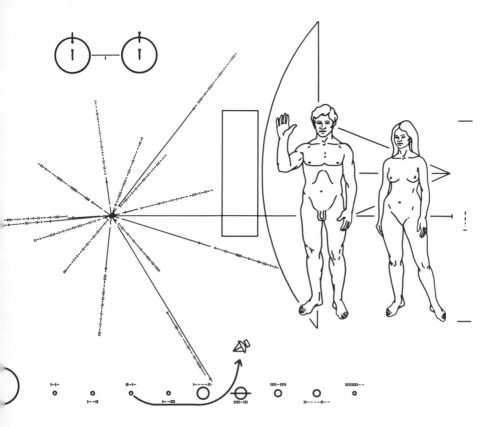

The Pioneer plaque designed by Carl Sagan and Frank Drake.

waves). The positions of the lines give directions and the length of the lines give relative distances. The frequencies of the pulsars are shown at the ends of the lines. Since the frequency rate of pulsars decreases with time, an alien society could determine the time elapsed since launch by the differences between pulse rate then and pulse rate at the time of recovery of the spacecraft.

At the bottom of the plaque is a crude diagram of the solar system, on which the launch site and route of Pioneer are indicated.

The man and woman at the right of the plaque indicate the kinds of creatures who launched the craft. Behind them is an outline drawing of a Pioneer to provide a size-scale for the figures. The man's hand is raised in what hopefully will be interpreted as a sign of friendship. The hand also shows five fingers, including the thumb, which is distinctively human—no other animal possesses one just like it.

Perhaps somewhere, sometime, creatures will wonder about Pioneer, the strange contraption that was found circling their planet. Those creatures may be thousands of light-years away, and they may be living several million years from now.

Nevertheless, some people believe we should not have put such a plaque aboard the Pioneers. Suppose, they say, those far-off civilizations become so curious about Earth that they launch an expedition to explore the planet? Suppose their motives are not friendly? Suppose they consider the creatures shown on the plaque as threats to be destroyed? The plaque, they say, may be an open invitation to our own destruction.

These people fail to realize that we revealed our presence a long time ago when television signals were first broadcast. Those waves continue into space. All that is needed is a sensitive receiver to pick them up. Then they can be converted into pictures. Can you imagine the wonder our old TV shows would cause on an alien world?

Fortunately, reason won over those few persons who had such objections. Even if an invasion should follow Pioneer's recovery, it would be millions of years from now. Very likely mankind will have disappeared from the

After passing Saturn, Voyager begins a journey of billions of kilometers around the Galaxy. A billion years from now it may encounter other creatures on other worlds out among the stars.

planet. Perhaps the planet itself will have disappeared, burned to a crisp as the Sun became a red giant star and expanded so much that the planet was surrounded by its hot gases.

VOYAGER

Just as the Pioneers journeyed into space between the stars, so also will the Voyagers. They will become cold, quiet, solitary objects speeding through endless space. But just in case they may be picked up by an alien civilization, the Voyagers carry information about Earth. The collection is much more complete than the data on the Pioneer plaque. It was decided to put a record aboard Voyager, a record containing sounds of Earth, and pictures that had been changed into coded sounds.

It was hard to decide what to include. Suppose you were asked to select those sounds that would be unique and could be understood by a civilization somewhere in the Galaxy that was advanced enough to travel among the stars. These are some of the sounds that were decided upon: volcanoes, earthquakes, thunder, wind and rain, crickets and frogs, birds, a screeching chimpanzee, heartbeats, laughter, sawing, airplanes, cars, and pulsars. One section of the record is devoted to greetings from Earth people, each in his or her own language—Greek, Russian, Thai, Hebrew, Spanish, Japanese, English, Zulu—altogether fifty-five languages are represented. There are greetings from people of the United Nations, as well as the Secretary-General of the United Nations, and from the President of the United States. Here is part of the President's message:

This is a present from a small distant world, a token of our sounds, our science, our images, our music, our thoughts, and our feelings. We are attempting to survive our time so we may live into yours. We hope someday, having solved the problems we face, to join a community of galactic civilizations. This record represents our hopes and our determinations and our good will in a vast and awesome universe.

The sounds also include several minutes of music. Selections have been made from the compositions of classical composers such as Bach, Beethoven, Mozart, Verdi, Ravel, Enesco, from American jazz, as well as from the music of Java, Japan, Russia, Bulgaria, Peru, the Navajos, New Guinea, and Australia.

In addition to sounds of Earth, the record also contains pictures that have been converted to sound. (The process is similar to the way video signals are changed into pictures.)

In all, there are 118 pictures. There were many problems deciding which ones to use, principally to select pictures that told a lot but were at the same time easy to understand. The first picture is simply a circle, then comes a picture of the Galaxy and the Sun's location at the center of pulsars (as in Pioneer). The pictures show the anatomy of humans, and there are photos of the planets, flowers, shells, people of many races, houses, cities, cars and roads, astronauts, et cetera.

Ways had to be found to direct the aliens who might pick up Voyager how to play the records and how to construct the pictures from the sounds. That information is on the aluminum cover of the record, which it is hoped will survive the space voyage. Etched on it are directions for playing the record and for producing the pictures from the audio messages. The stylus (which is aboard the craft) and cartridge are shown in the correct position for playing the record, in both top and side views.

Fastened to the cover is a pure source of uranium 238, which is 2 centimeters in diameter. The steady decay of the uranium into other substances makes it into a clock. In 4.51 billion years, half of the uranium will decay into other elements. By comparing the amount of uranium and decay products, an alien scientist could figure out the age of the sample and so of Voyager. This information could be used for checking conclusions about time made from the frequency rates of the pulsars on the cover.

SURVIVAL OF VOYAGER

Space is far from empty. The inner solar system contains hordes of micrometeorites. These are small bits of matter, probably debris left as comets were pulled apart by the Sun's gravitation. The abundance drops off in the outer part of the solar system, and it is probably small indeed in deep space, between the stars.

Nevertheless, one must assume that micrometeorites will strike the record. It is fastened to the outside of Voyager, where it is open to bombardment. However, the record is inside an aluminum case and so it should be able to withstand considerable bombarding. Some damage has already occurred to Voyager during its journey to Jupiter. Probably a fraction of 1 percent of the surface area, if any, was affected. In interstellar space the damage would be much slower. Most scientists think the Voyager records will have a lifetime of a billion years. That estimate would be reduced if Voyager were to enter the inner region of another solar system, one that also contained debris of long-gone comets.

No one knows if such systems exist, but it is possible. The presence of one is suspected around Barnard's star, a star that is smaller than the Sun and cooler. Another such star is in the Little Dipper. Just as there seem to be planets around Barnard's star, there may be planets here. Voyager may be directed toward that star. At some far-off time, an alien civilization may recover Voyager, decipher the code, and reproduce the sounds and pictures of Earth. They are messages for eternity.

Some Facts About Jupiter

Diameter at equator   142 900 km

Radius at equator   71 450 km

Circumference at equator   449 110 km

Period of rotation on axis   9.85 hours

Equatorial speed rotation   45 000 km/h

Period of revolution around the Sun   11.86 Earth years

Distance of revolution around the Sun   5000 million km

Inclination of orbit   1.3 degrees (Earth zero)

Oblateness (flattening)   0.062 (Earth 0.0033)

Albedo (percent of light reflected)   0.44

Volume   1300 (Earth = 1)

Surface area   125 (Earth = 1)

Apparent motion   300″ / 24 hours (6.2 days to move width of
                  the Moon)

Average speed in orbit   13.1 km/s (Earth 29.8)

Maximum distance from Sun   5.45 a.u. (astronomical unit is
the distance between Earth
and Sun)
Minimum distance from Sun   4.95 a.u.
Average distance from Sun   5.20 a.u.
779 million km
(Earth 150 million km)
Density   1.34 g/cm^3 (Earth — 5.52 g/cm^3)
Mass   318.4 (Earth = 1)
Temperature   (Cloud tops) −120 ° C
(Interior) 60 000 ° C

Conversion Table

THE METRIC SYSTEM OF MEASUREMENT USES,
meters for length
grams for mass (weight at sea levels)
liters for volume

TO CONVERT ENGLISH MEASUREMENTS TO METRIC,
OR METRIC TO ENGLISH:
1 inch = 2.54 centimeters
1 foot = 0.305 meters
1 yard = 0.014 meters
1 mile = 1.609 kilometers
1 pound = 0.454 kilograms
1 quart = 0.946 liter
1 centimeter = 0.3937 inch
1 meter = 39.37 inches
1 kilometer = 0.621 mile
1 gram = 0.035 ounce
1 kilogram = 2.20 pounds
1 liter = 1.06 quarts

Further Reading

Asimov, Isaac, *Jupiter, the Largest Planet,* rev. ed. New York: Lothrop, Lee and Shepard Co., 1976.

Branley, Franklyn M., *The Nine Planets,* rev. ed. New York: Thomas Y. Crowell, 1978.

Branley, Franklyn M., et al., *Astronomy.* New York: Thomas Y. Crowell, 1975.

Gore, Rick, "What Voyager Saw: Jupiter's Dazzling Realm," *National Geographic,* Vol. 157, No. 1 (January 1980), pp. 2–29.

Hartmann, Wm. K., "Moons of the Outer Solar System," *Smithsonian* (January 1980), pp. 36–46

Sagan, Carl, et al., *Murmurs of Earth.* New York: Ballantine Books, 1978.

Shurkin, Joel N., *Jupiter: The Star That Failed.* Philadelphia: the Westminster Press, 1979.

Soderblom, Laurence A., "The Galilean Moons of Jupiter," *Scientific American* (January 1980).

NASA, *Galileo to Jupiter.* Jet Propulsion Lab., California Institute of Technology, Pasadena (July 1979).

NASA, *Voyager Encounters Jupiter.* Jet Propulsion Lab., California Institute of Technology, Pasadena (July 1979).

"Reports on Voyager 2," *Science,* Vol. 206, No. 4421 (November 23, 1979), pp. 925–996.

INDEX

About the author

Franklyn M. Branley, Astronomer Emeritus and former Chairman of The American Museum-Hayden Planetarium, is well known as the author of many books about astronomy and other sciences for young people of all ages.

Dr. Branley holds degrees from New York University, Columbia University, and the State University of New York College at New Paltz. He and his wife live in Sag Harbor, New York.